A Reader's
Theater Script
and
Guide

一看就
少儿英语小剧场

王子与公主

主　编　杜效明
副主编　闵　璇
编　委　潘晨曦　凌　凝　杨德俊　周莹莹　张玉霞
　　　　张文慧　慕媛媛　吴　昊　赵　芹　吴秀玲
　　　　冯　会　余晓琴　都兰芳

APETIME
时代出版
时代出版传媒股份有限公司
安徽科学技术出版社

图书在版编目(CIP)数据

王子与公主 / 杜效明主编.--合肥:安徽科学技术出版社,2022.1

(一看就会演的少儿英语小剧场)

ISBN 978-7-5337-8463-8

Ⅰ.①王… Ⅱ.①杜… Ⅲ.①英语-少儿读物 Ⅳ.①H319.4

中国版本图书馆 CIP 数据核字(2021)第 123018 号

WANGZI YU GONGZHU

王 子 与 公 主

主 编 杜效明

副主编 闵 璇

出 版 人:丁凌云 选题策划:张 雯 周璟瑜 责任编辑:郑 楠
责任校对:岑红宇 责任印制:廖小青 装帧设计:武 迪
出版发行:时代出版传媒股份有限公司 http://www.press-mart.com
安徽科学技术出版社 http://www.ahstp.net
(合肥市政务文化新区翡翠路 1118 号出版传媒广场,邮编:230071)
电话:(0551)63533330
印 制:合肥锦华印务有限公司 电话:(0551)65539314
(如发现印装质量问题,影响阅读,请与印刷厂商联系调换)

开本:710×1010 1/16 印张:5.5 字数:110 千
版次:2022 年 1 月第 1 版 2022 年 1 月第 1 次印刷

ISBN 978-7-5337-8463-8 定价:28.00 元

推荐序

　　"一看就会演的少儿英语小剧场"系列图书是一套以英语短剧为表现形式的双语读物，选编了8个家喻户晓的童话故事，故事幽默诙谐，富有戏剧性；语言地道，童趣盎然，并提供发音纯正的音频，带来真实、生动的情境体验。

　　本系列图书集自主阅读、分角色朗读、戏剧表演等多种功能于一体，学生可以通过剧本诵读、戏剧表演和贯穿其中的互动合作，获得语言感知、语言理解、语言运用和语言鉴赏的多种体验，在语言、情感、思维、文化意识等多方面获得整体提升。

　　英语小剧场是一场由想象力构建的活动，它和普通而枯燥的死记硬背型阅读活动有本质区别。《义务教育英语课程标准》提出，小学生除了简单的听、说、读、写，还应能够进行英语表演。生动有趣的戏剧表演已成为一种以文学作品的口述演绎为中心的综合语言艺术活动。语言在戏剧中是不可或缺的元素，作家通过语言表达戏剧的立意和冲突，演员通过台词表达人物的思想和精神，导演也必须帮助演员处理台词。古希腊时期，许多知名的政治家都要拜演员为师，向演员学习台词功夫，以便提高他们的演说水平。声、台、形、表，基本功对表演艺术来说是缺一不可的，因此演员要具备声乐艺术、语言艺术、舞蹈艺术和表演艺术的修养。作为一种听、说、读、写、思全面发展的活动体验，戏剧表演对学生的英语语言学习和综合素质的提升起到了独特的作用，有助于提高学生的主动阅读能力、批判性思考能力、创意写作能力、精确表达能力、专注倾听能力以及高效的协作能力。

戏剧艺术既是综合艺术（时间和空间艺术的综合），也是集体艺术，需要集体协作才能完成。英国教育学家约翰内森和卡恩认为："运用小组协作的方式来促成学生之间更高级、更深层的互动，这一点尤其重要。"小剧场的表演形式使学生围绕着一个共同的目标进行团队协作，他们可以就内容、角色、舞台表演等细节进行充分讨论沟通。戏剧表演给学生提供了可以广泛参与的学习模式，丰富学生的实践经历，提高学生的团队合作能力。

对于教师而言，也需要一些创新、不同寻常的项目应用于课堂实践。本书中生动有趣的英语短剧，融合了极具时代感的语言表达；随书附赠的《阅读指导》手册，为教师提供具有实操性的说明和指导，帮助策划、实施并完成一场别开生面的戏剧表演活动，开展新颖有趣的第二课堂。学生们可以投入极大的热情且无须耗费太多精力，在相对较短的时间内即可产出一部成熟的舞台作品。本系列图书熔素质教育和英语教学于一炉，是小学英语教学实践的应用范例。

导读

你爱不爱做道具？有没有兴趣来画布景呢？你喜欢表演吗？如果是的话，那么就来排场话剧吧。话剧多有趣啊！话剧是让孩子们学会团队合作的最好的方法！

读者剧场的形式最简单。小读者坐在舞台的椅子上，他们不用背台词，只要把对话有感情地朗读出来便成功啦！

朗读剧场和一般的舞台剧有点儿像。演员们不仅要化装、穿戏服，还要在台上走位，一边说台词一边表演。不过，演员全程是可以看台词的。除此之外，舞台上还要搭布景、放道具。

读者剧场的台本还可以用作木偶剧。小演员站在台幕后，一边移动木偶，一边读对话。

定下话剧形式后，你首先要找到一个足够大的空间来表演。小礼堂的舞台是个不错的选择哟！当然，你也可以在教室里演出。接下来，你要初步定下演出的日期，提交使用舞台的申请。然后，为你的演出做些宣传吧。你可以把宣传单或海报张贴到学校或者社区的布告栏里。

别忘了把这个消息告诉朋友和家人哟！大家都会很期待你的表演的！

show出你的发音
争当英语小明星
▶ 地道口语课
▶ 剧本推荐
微信扫码

目录

英语·小·剧场
展示大舞台

show出你的发音，争当英语小明星

跟我说 ★ **地道口语课**

实用外教口语定制课程，标准英语脱口而出

跟我听 ★ **剧本推荐**

精听好剧本，带你"真听真看真感受"

微信扫码
还可获取本书推荐书单
好书读不停！

门票和剧目单

你可以亲手制作门票和剧目单，也可以用电脑设计它们。不论你选择哪种方法，一定要确定门票上标有剧名、演出日期和具体时间，以及演出地点。

剧目单上应列有节目顺序。剧目单的正面一般印有剧名和演出时间。演员及工作人员的姓名要放在剧目单内页。记得要准备足够的剧目单，并在开演之前把它们发给入场的观众哟。

演员和舞台工作人员

　　一场话剧需要很多人的参与。首先，让我们来分配角色。剧组的每个演员都要配有剧本，并且要熟练地掌握自己的台词。一遍遍地高声朗读你的台词可以让你更快地找到感觉。

　　接下来，需要招工作人员了。一场话剧没有这些重要的工作人员怎么行呢！一个人是可以负责多项工作的。

总导演：管理人员，布置任务。

服装设计师：借道具、做服装。

舞台监督：保障每个环节顺利进行。

灯光设计师：负责打聚光灯和换光。

布景师：设计、制作布景。

道具师：筹备、制作、管理道具。

特效工作人员：负责音效和特效。

妆容和服装

　　化妆师的工作是整场演出的重中之重！每个参与的演员都是要化妆的，不过，舞台演员化的妆要比我们日常生活中化得浓一点儿。你手边要有基本的彩妆用品，比如睫毛膏、粉底液、腮红和口红等。可以用一次性化妆棉或化妆用棉签给演员上妆，要保证卫生哟！

　　服装设计师需要按照剧情设计服装。他们负责借服装，或者按照每个角色对旧衣服进行改造。借服装或者制作演出服时，你也可以向家长寻求帮助。

布景和道具

　　在读者剧场中，道具就是椅子，演员只需要坐在最前面就可以了。相比之下，朗读剧场和一般的舞台剧可就不是这么简单了，布景和道具是必不可少的。

　　布景是为每一幕布置的景物。

　　道具是演员在演出时需要用到的器物。

排演安排和舞台方位

一旦做出上演话剧的决定，就要制作一张彩排时间表喽，并协调大家的时间，尽量在公演之前彩排五次吧。

即便你只需要按照剧本读台词，但是，作为一个团队，你们还是要一起练习。熟练掌握自己的台词后，舞台表演才能更加流畅、自然。没有台词的时候，只要演员还留在台上，就需要做出符合自己角色的动作和表情。

剧本里的舞台方位是从演员的角度得出的，被标注在括号内。表演时，你要面向观众席，所以，左边指的就是你的左手边，右边指的就是你的右手边。

有些舞台术语可能让你摸不着头脑，比如

大幕：舞台的主要幕布，在台口内。

观众席：观众的座位。

侧幕：舞台的左、右边，是藏在观众视线之外的舞台的侧面。

故事剧场一

白雪公主与怪杰七兄弟

布景和道具

　　布景: 用硬纸板做的城堡放在舞台正位, 配上用硬纸板做的森林或者几棵假树。最后一幕发生在怪杰七兄弟的家里, 所以, 要放上几张电脑桌和几台台式电脑。问问你的学校有没有老式的台式电脑和键盘, 可以借来用一用。在地板上放被子和枕头当作七张床。怪杰兄弟的屋里还要有一张桌子和七把椅子, 七兄弟在这里吃早饭。

　　道具: 你可以用一个空画框或者硬纸板来当魔镜, 利蒂西娅王后需要一个装有红苹果的篮子, 怪杰兄弟的餐桌上还要放些塑料或纸质餐盘。用海报纸或者美工纸做出一张巨大的红嘴唇, 并把它粘在上好色的木棍上。

演员表

旁白：讲故事的人。

白雪公主：一位美丽的小公主。

国王：白雪公主的父亲。

利蒂西娅王后：一个坏巫婆。

魔镜：利蒂西娅王后的镜子，它拥有魔力。

怪杰兄弟：六兄弟是电脑怪才，他们是老大"坏脾气"、老二"慢吞吞"，老三"邋遢虫"，老四"呆头脑"，老五"小胖墩"，老小"神经质"。

霍华德：六兄弟收留的新弟兄。

9

妆容和服装

旁白：衬衫和裤子，配披肩。

白雪公主：王冠配长裙，在森林一幕中需要配一件披风。

国王：王冠配华丽的衬衫。

利蒂西娅王后：王冠配长裙，扮成卖苹果的老婆婆时需要配一件披风。

魔镜：黑衣、黑裤；扮演魔镜的人手握空画框或中间被挖空的硬纸板，这样观众就可以透过画框或纸板看到他的脸了。

怪杰兄弟：老大"坏脾气"、老二"慢吞吞"、老三"邋遢虫"、老四"呆头脑"、老五"小胖墩"、老小"神经质"身着同款短衫，戴着滑稽的帽子或者大眼镜。他们每个人的脖子上都挂着写有名字的标签牌。

霍华德：和怪杰兄弟衣着相同，另配一顶假发或者帽子。

show出你的发音
争当英语小明星
▶ 地道口语课
▶ 剧本推荐

微信扫码

舞台方位

右侧幕区

左侧幕区

上舞台右侧

上舞台中心

上舞台左侧

舞台正位右侧

舞台正位

舞台正位左侧

下舞台右侧

下舞台中心

下舞台左侧

Script: Snow White and the Seven Dorks

Scene 1: The Castle

(Opening of the Curtain: Snow White sits alone reading on a chair at center stage. The narrator sits on a stool at stage right removed from the action.)

Narrator: *(Points at Snow White)* Once upon a time, a beautiful princess named Snow White lived with her father, the king. They lived in an awesome castle on the edge of a lake. Her mother, the queen, had passed away some years before. One day, the king went away on a long trip. When he returned he brought back a new wife.

King: *(King enters with Queen Leticia.)* Snow White, this is my new wife, Queen Leticia. She will be your stepmother.

Snow White: *(Stands and bows)* Welcome to our castle!

Queen Leticia: *(Coldly)* Thank you, Snow White.

Snow White: I will ask the cook to prepare a special dinner in your honor! Any woman my father loves must be a very good woman.

(Snow White and the king exit.)

Narrator: But Snow White was wrong. Queen Leticia was really a beautiful witch, who had charmed the king into marrying her. *(The Magic Mirror enters.)* On Queen Leticia's first day, she set up her magic mirror. She asked it the question she asked it every morning.

Queen Leticia: *(Faces mirror)* Mirror, Mirror, look at me. Am I the loveliest that you see?

Mirror: Your beauty was beyond compare. But now another is more fair.

Queen Leticia: *(Angrily)* What? I don't believe you! How could anyone be more beautiful than me?

Mirror: Snow White is pure and good and true. She's far more beautiful than you.

Queen Leticia: *(Stamping her foot)* No one more beautiful than me will be allowed to live in this kingdom!

I will make Snow White's life miserable! Then maybe she will leave and I will have the king to myself. *(Queen exits.)*

剧本：白雪公主与怪杰七兄弟

第一幕：城堡

（大幕拉开：白雪公主独自一人坐在舞台正位的椅子上看书。旁白坐在舞台正位右侧，远离演员。）

旁白：（手指白雪公主）很久很久以前，有一位美丽的公主，她和她的国王父亲住在湖边富丽堂皇的城堡里，她就是白雪公主。白雪公主的母亲几年前过世了。这天，出访数日的国王回来了。和他一起回来的，还有他新娶的妻子。

国王：（国王和利蒂西娅王后一起上场。）白雪公主，来，见见我的新妻子——利蒂西娅王后。她就是你的继母了。

白雪公主：（起身，躬身行礼）请允许我代表整个城堡欢迎您！

利蒂西娅王后：（冷冰冰地）谢谢你，白雪公主。

白雪公主：我去叫厨师专门为您准备一份特别的大餐！我父亲爱上的女人一定是全天下最善良的人。

（白雪公主和国王下场。）

旁白：然而，白雪公主想错了。利蒂西娅王后其实是个漂亮的女巫，国王中了她的魔法，才娶了她。（魔镜上台。）利蒂西娅王后入住城堡的第一天，就唤来了魔镜。她又提出了那个她每天早上都要问的问题。

利蒂西娅王后：（面向魔镜）魔镜，魔镜，看着我，我是不是世界上最美丽的女人？

魔镜：您是绝世佳人。不过，还有一个人比您更美丽。

利蒂西娅王后：（生气地）什么？我才不信你的话呢！怎么可能有人比我美？

魔镜：白雪公主不仅心地纯真，而且美丽动人。她的美胜过您的千倍。

利蒂西娅王后：（跺脚）这个王国里不能有比我还美的人！我要让白雪公主度日如年！这样，她就会走人了，她走了以后，国王就是我一个人的啦！（利蒂西娅王后下场。）

Scene 2: Inside the Castle

Scene change: Stage crew closes curtain and replaces the castle with a forest. Scene two is performed in front of the closed curtain.

(Snow White is on her knees scrubbing the floor.)

Narrator: And so, Queen Leticia made Snow White's life miserable. She gave away all of her beautiful clothes and made the princess dress in rags.

Snow White: I look like a beggar in these clothes. Now, I eat in the kitchen and work like a servant.

Narrator: And worst of all, Queen Leticia banished Snow White's boyfriend, Prince Rupert, from the kingdom.

Snow White: *(Crying)* My father doesn't even notice how she treats me. I have no one left who I can trust. Tomorrow, I will run away and find Prince Rupert! *(Snow White exits.)*

第二幕：城堡里

换布景：舞台工作人员拉上大幕，将城堡换成森林。第二幕在合上的大幕前表演。

（白雪公主跪在地上擦地板。）

旁白：正如王后所言，她让白雪公主的生活变得悲惨不堪。她拿走了小公主所有漂亮的衣服，还给她穿得破破烂烂的。

白雪公主：我穿得就像个乞丐。现在，连饭都得在厨房里吃，每天像个仆人似的忙来忙去。

旁白：更糟糕的是，利蒂西娅王后把白雪公主的男朋友——鲁珀特王子，赶出了王国。

白雪公主：（哭泣着说）我父亲竟然没有发现她这么折磨我。我身边连一个可以信任的人都没有了。明天，我要逃离这个地方，去找我的鲁珀特王子！（白雪公主下场。）

Scene 3: The Froest

Scene change: *The curtain opens to show the forest.*

Narrator: The next night, Snow White waited until the castle was dark and quiet. She packed a few things and set off into the forest.

Snow White: *(Snow White enters.)* I've never been this far from the castle before. I'm so scared!

Narrator: Now, it was winter and the night was very cold. Soon, small snowflakes drifted down. Snow White was hopelessly lost.

(Stage crew can throw small bits of white paper or fake snowflakes on the stage around Snow White.)

Snow White: I am so cold. I don't know what to do. *(Walks slowly across the stage)*

Narrator: As she wandered, she saw a light through the trees. As she came closer, she saw it was a little cottage

with satellite dishes on the roof. Snow White knocked at the door.

Snow White: *(Pretends to knock at an imaginary door. Sound crew makes knocking noise)* Oh, I hope a kind person will let me come in!

第三幕：森林里

换背景：大幕拉开，森林出现。

旁白：第二天晚上，白雪公主等待城堡上下的灯都灭了，所有的人都睡着了，才带着她收拾好的东西，逃向了森林。

白雪公主：（白雪公主上场。）我从来没有离开城堡走得这么远过，我好害怕！

旁白：现在正值冬季，夜晚格外寒冷。很快，天上飘下了雪花。白雪公主彻底迷失了方向。

（工作人员可以把白纸屑或者假的雪花撒在白雪公主身边。）

白雪公主：我冷极了，现在该怎么办啊？（慢慢地穿过舞台）

旁白：就在她穿过森林的时候，她隐约看到了远处的灯光。白雪公主走近一看，是一栋小屋，屋顶上还有圆盘式卫星电视天线。白雪公主敲了敲门。

白雪公主：（做出敲门的动作，音效组做出叩门声）天哪，真希望好心人可以让我进去取取暖！

show出你的发音
争当英语小明星
▸ 地道口语课
▸ 剧本推荐

微信扫码

Scene 4: The Dork's House

Scene change: The curtain closes for set up of the Dorks' house. Scene opens with all the dorks except Grumpy sleeping on the floor with their pillows and blankets.

Grumpy: Who's there? Do you realize how late it is?

Snow White: It's Snow White. Can I come in, please?

Grumpy: Just a minute, I'm logging off.

Narrator: When the door opened, Snow White saw a strange little man. The room was filled with computers. Wires ran all over the floor. She stepped inside.

Grumpy: Hi, I'm Grumpy. You've reached the Dork Squad. Are you having trouble with your computer?

Snow White: I don't have a computer.

Grumpy: Then why are you here? All we do is fix computers.

Snow White: I'm lost. I'm looking for somewhere to spend the night.

Grumpy: Well, the house is kind of full already. I live here with my six brothers: Lumpy, Frumpy, Chumpy, Dumpy, Jumpy, and Howard.

Snow White: Could I stay just for tonight? It's snowing outside.

Grumpy: Well, I suppose so. I'll be up all night. I'm taking the late shift. My bed's right over there. I'll just get back to my computers.

Snow White: You're very kind.

 Narrator: Snow White spent the night at the Dork Squad's house. In the morning, she got up very early and fixed a nice breakfast. The dorks wakened to the smell of bread baking, bacon frying, and eggs cooking. They were surprised to see Snow White in their kitchen.

(Snow White walks in from stage right and puts plates out on the table. The Dorks sit up and stretch and yawn.)

Lumpy: Something smells really good! (He stands up and sees Snow White.) Oh, who are you?

Grumpy: This is Snow White. She was lost in the forest last night.

Lumpy: Hi, Snow White! Where do you live? I'd be glad to help you find your way home.

Snow White: I don't want to go home.

All Dorks: Why not?

(The Dorks sit down at the table while the narrator is talking.)

Narrator: So, Snow White told the seven dorks all about her new stepmother and how she didn't want to live at the castle anymore.

Chumpy: Why don't you just live with us, Snow White? This food is fantastic!

Frumpy: We could use someone to take care of us. We spend all our time fixing computers. It would be nice to have a hot meal every once in a while.

Dumpy: I'll even give you my bed. We all sleep on the floor anyway. Why don't you stay?

Snow White: Well, all right, I will stay here. Thank you very much!

(All Dorks exit except Grumpy, who sits down at one of the computers. Snow White clears the table.)

Narrator: So every day, Snow White cooked and baked and kept the little house tidy for her new friends. At night, the Dorks taught her all about computers and the Internet. All except Howard, who just looked very sad and never said anything at all. Finally, Snow White asked Grumpy about Howard.

Snow White: What's the matter with Howard?

Grumpy: I don't know. We think he is under a spell. He hasn't talked since he came here.

Snow White: But I thought he was one of your brothers.

Grumpy: We found him wandering in the forest. We adopted him.

Snow White: You adopted me, too. You Dorks are just the best! *(Snow White gives Grumpy a hug.)*

(Grumpy exits. Snow White sits down to read a book.)

Narrator: One day, all seven dorks went to a technology conference. They left Snow White alone for three days. They warned her about not opening the door to strangers and locking the house at night. Snow White didn't have to cook or bake very much since the Dorks were away, so she decided to surf the Internet.

Snow White: Oh! I discovered this great Web site. Maybe if I make my own page, Prince Rupert will see it and try to contact me.

Narrator: Snow White put the Dorks' address and phone number on her new page. She spent all afternoon and evening on the computer hoping to receive some information from Prince Rupert. Late the next afternoon, there was a knock at the door.

Snow White: Oh, maybe that is Prince

Rupert! Who's there?

Queen Leticia: *(Disguising her voice)* Just an old woman selling winter apples, my dear. Would you like some?

Snow White: I would love some apples! I'd like to bake a pie for the seven Dorks. They have been so kind to me.

Narrator: Snow White didn't realize that the old woman was really her stepmother. Queen Leticia had seen Snow White's page. She was angry that Snow White still lived in the kingdom and she had come to give her a poisoned apple. *(Snow White opens the door.)*

Queen Leticia: *(Holds out an apple)* Here, my dear. Just taste one of these lovely apples.

Snow White: They are beautiful and red. They look very tasty!

Narrator: Snow White took a bite of the

apple and immediately fell to the floor in a deep sleep. *(Snow White collapses on the floor.)*

(Queen walks off the stage and exits.)

Narrator: It was early the next morning before the seven little men returned. *(Dorks enter and stand around Snow White.)* They found Snow White lying as still as death on the floor with the poisoned apple beside her.

Grumpy: Oh no, I think she ate a poisoned apple!

Chumpy: I'll bet Queen Leticia was here! What should we do?

Lumpy: What's the cure for poisoned apples?

Dumpy: Check the Internet!

Narrator: So Chumpy looked online.

Chumpy: It says she needs a kiss from her true love.

Jumpy: And who would that be?

Narrator: Just then Howard stepped forward. *(Howard holds up the giant lips on the paint stick and touches Snow White's mouth with them.)* He leaned over and kissed Snow White right on the lips. The Dorks were amazed!

Frumpy: Howard!

Lumpy: Wow! That was some kiss!

Jumpy: I didn't even know you liked her!

Grumpy: Look, Snow White's waking up! Maybe she'll be okay!

Narrator: Just as Snow White was beginning to rub her eyes and sit up, Howard began to look a little different. *(Howard takes off his wig or hat.)* He was smiling and his eyes twinkled. He looked just like Snow White's boyfriend, Prince Rupert. Snow White was delighted!

Snow White: Prince Rupert, I found you, at last!

Grumpy: I'm confused. You mean Howard was Prince Rupert all along?

Howard: Snow White's stepmother put a spell on me. She changed the way I looked and I couldn't talk! I could never tell anyone what had happened to me.

Chumpy: Wow! Snow White's stepmother was a meanie!

Grumpy: I don't understand how Queen Leticia found you, Snow White. We tried so hard to protect you.

Snow White: It's all my fault. I made a Web page to try to find Prince Rupert.

Lumpy: Didn't we tell you that anyone can read that stuff?

Frumpy: You have to be very careful what you post online!

Snow White: I know. I'm sorry. But now I don't need it anymore! I have Prince Rupert back.

Lumpy: I read online that the queen was deported for identity theft. You can go back to the castle and live with your father and Prince Rupert!

Snow White: But, I will miss you. I have an idea! Why don't you come to live at the castle? I think my father needs the Dork Squad to bring his kingdom into the twenty-first century! *(Everyone exits except the narrator.)*

Narrator: And so Snow White went home to live with her father, who had missed her very much. In a few years, she married Prince Rupert. The Dork Squad set up shop in the east tower with a cutting-edge security system. It had a special Queen Leticia detector to keep everyone safe. And they all lived happily ever after!

The End

第四幕：电脑怪杰兄弟家

换布景：台幕拉上，布置电脑怪杰兄弟的房间。大幕再拉开时，除了老大"坏脾气"，其余所有的兄弟都盖着被子，头枕在枕头上，睡在地上。

老大"坏脾气"：谁在门外呢？你知不知道现在几点了？

白雪公主：我是白雪公主。可不可以让我进来？求求你了。

老大"坏脾气"：等一下，我先退下网。

旁白：门一打开，一个有点儿怪的小矮个儿站在了公主面前。屋里全是电脑，电线凌乱地缠绕在地板各处。白雪公主进了屋。

老大"坏脾气"：嘿，你好，我是"坏脾气"。你现在进入的是"电脑怪杰兄弟智囊团"的领地。你的电脑出了什么问题呢？

白雪公主：我没有电脑。

老大"坏脾气"：咦，那你到这儿来做什么？我们只提供维修电脑的服务。

白雪公主：我迷路了。我想找个地方过夜。

老大"坏脾气"：这样啊，不过，这个房子有点儿挤。

我和我的六个兄弟都住在这儿：老二"慢吞吞"，老

三"邋遢虫"，老四"呆头脑"，老五"小胖墩"，

老小"神经质"，还有霍华德。

白雪公主：我可不可以就待一晚上？外面下着雪呢。

老大"坏脾气"：嗯……我觉得应该没问题吧。我今

晚上夜班，不睡觉。我的床就在那边，你去休息吧。

我得去看电脑了。

白雪公主：你真是太好了。

旁白：于是，白雪公主待在了电脑怪杰兄弟智囊团的

家过夜。早晨，她很早就起了床，为这家人准备了一

桌美味的早餐。烤面包、煎培根和煮鸡蛋的香味把其

余的几个兄弟馋醒了。大家惊讶地看着站在他们的厨

房里的白雪公主。

（白雪公主从舞台右侧上场，把手中的盘子摆放在桌

子上。电脑怪杰兄弟伸着懒腰、打着哈欠起床了。）

老二"慢吞吞"：什么东西这么好闻啊！（他起床看

到了白雪公主。）嘿，你是谁啊？

老大"坏脾气"：这是白雪公主。她昨晚在森林里迷路了。

老二"慢吞吞"：你好，白雪公主！你住在哪里呢？如果能帮助你找到回家的路，我会很高兴的。

白雪公主：可是，我不想回家。

所有的电脑怪杰兄弟齐声问：为什么不想回家？

（旁白继续的时候，所有兄弟都围坐在桌前。）

旁白：白雪公主就将她的遭遇告诉了这七兄弟，也告诉了他们自己不想再在城堡里住下去的原因。

老四"呆头脑"：要不然，你就跟我们住在一起吧，白雪公主。你做的饭太好吃了！

老三"邋遢虫"：你可以当我们的女管家。我们把所有时间都用来修电脑，没有时间照顾自己。要是时不时能吃上热饭该多好啊！

老五"小胖墩"：我把我的床让给你吧。我们总是睡在地板上，没关系的。你留下来吧！

白雪公主：好吧，那就这么定了，我会留下来的。太谢谢你们了！

（除了老大"坏脾气"，其余的兄弟退场。老大"坏脾气"坐在一台电脑前。白雪公主在擦桌子。）

旁白：就这样，白天，白雪公主为这七个新朋友做饭、烘烤、打扫房间。到了晚上，电脑怪杰兄弟教她使用电脑和上网。只有霍华德看上去总是那么伤心，沉默不语。终于有一天，白雪公主向老大"坏脾气"问起了霍华德。

白雪公主：霍华德怎么了？

老大"坏脾气"：我们也不知道发生了什么。估计他被诅咒了。自打到这儿来，他就没开口说过话。

白雪公主：哦，原来是这样啊，我还以为他也是你们的兄弟呢。

老大"坏脾气"：我们在森林里发现了他，他独自一人游荡，我们就收留了他。

白雪公主：你们也收留了我。你们兄弟是最善良的！

（白雪公主给了老大"坏脾气"一个大大的拥抱。）

（老大"坏脾气"退场。白雪公主坐下读书。）

旁白：一天，电脑怪杰七兄弟要离家三天去参加一个技术会议。他们把白雪公主独自留在家。七兄弟告诫她，不要给陌生人开门，并叮嘱她晚上一定要锁好大门。电脑怪杰兄弟离家的这几天，白雪公主不用忙着做饭了，她决定，正好用这个时间上网看看。

白雪公主：喔！我找到了这个网站，看起来真棒。我没准可以建一个自己的网页，这样鲁珀特王子看到后，就可以试着找到我了。

旁白：白雪公主说做就做，她花了整个下午和晚上，给自己建了一个网页，上面写有电脑怪杰兄弟的住址和电话号码，她希望有一天可以收到鲁珀特王子的消息。第二天下午，太阳快落山的时候，有人敲响了电脑怪杰兄弟家的大门。

白雪公主：哦，没准是鲁珀特王子来了！谁啊？

利蒂西娅王后：（变了声音）亲爱的孩子，我是卖苹果的老太婆，你要不要买些好吃的苹果啊？

白雪公主：我挺想买点儿苹果的！这样的话，我就可以给七兄弟烤苹果蛋糕啦。他们对我实在太好了。

旁白：白雪公主根本没有发现，那个老太婆其实就是她的继母。利蒂西娅王后看到了白雪公主的网页后，气急败坏，她无法忍受白雪公主还在这个王国里的事实。她带着毒苹果来到了白雪公主的住处。(白雪公主打开了门。)

利蒂西娅王后:(拿出一个苹果)亲爱的孩子,拿着。先尝一个美味的苹果吧。

白雪公主:它们又红又大。看上去很好吃!

旁白:白雪公主咬了一口苹果后,立刻倒在地上昏睡过去。(白雪公主倒在地上。)

(利蒂西娅王后穿过舞台下场。)

旁白:第二天一大早,电脑怪杰七兄弟回到了家。(七兄弟上台,站在白雪公主旁边。)他们发现了躺在地上、一动不动的白雪公主,旁边就是那颗毒苹果。

老大"坏脾气":哦,天哪!她可能吃了有毒的苹果了!

老四"呆头脑":我敢肯定利蒂西娅王后到这儿来过了!我们该怎么办呀?

老二"慢吞吞":怎么解这个毒呢?

老五"小胖墩":快上网查查!

旁白:老四"呆头脑"迅速上网查了起来。

老四"呆头脑":网上说,只要得到真爱之吻,她就能活过来了。

老二"慢吞吞"：那，谁是她的真爱呢？

旁白：话音未落，霍华德就向前迈了一步。(霍华德用贴在木棍上的巨大的嘴唇，点了一下白雪公主的嘴唇。)他弯腰亲了白雪公主的嘴唇。其他兄弟惊讶万分！

老三"邋遢虫"：天哪，霍华德！

老二"慢吞吞"：喔！好甜的吻哟！

老幺"神经质"：我之前没发现你喜欢她啊！

老大"坏脾气"：快看，白雪公主醒过来啦！她可能没事啦！

旁白：就在白雪公主揉着眼睛坐起来的时候，霍华德的模样发生了变化。(霍华德摘去假发或者帽子。)他的脸上出现了微笑，眼睛也比以前更有神了。他看起来很像白雪公主的男朋友——鲁珀特王子。白雪公主顿时高兴极了！

白雪公主：哦，鲁珀特王子，我终于找到你了！

老大"坏脾气"：我有点儿糊涂了。也就是说，鲁珀特王子是霍华德？

霍华德：白雪公主的继母给我下了咒。她改变了我的样子，还让我说不出话来！我根本没法告诉大家究竟发生了什么。

老四"呆头脑"：哈！白雪公主的继母就是个大坏蛋！

老大"坏脾气"：我现在还有件事搞不清楚：利蒂西娅王后是怎么找到你的呢？我们那么努力地保护你，不让她发现你的行踪。

白雪公主：都是我不好。因为我想找到鲁珀特王子，所以，我给自己建了个网页。

老二"慢吞吞"：我们不是告诉过你，所有的人都能看到你在网上发的信息吗？

老三"邋遢虫"：你要小心不能在网上乱写啊！

白雪公主：你们说的对。真对不起，没有听你们的劝告。从今天起，我再也不需要这个网页了！我找到鲁珀特王子啦。

老二"慢吞吞"：我刚刚在网上看到，王后因为盗用身份被驱逐出国了。你可以回到城堡，和你的父亲、鲁珀特王子重新生活在一起啦！

白雪公主：太好了，不过，我舍不得你们。我有个主意！你们和我一起住到城堡里，怎么样？我父亲可能需要电脑怪杰兄弟智囊团来带领他的国家进入二十一世纪呀！

(全体演员下场，只留旁白一人在台上。)

旁白：就这样，白雪公主回到了家，她的父亲望眼欲穿地盼到了女儿的归来，他们又快乐地生活在一起了。几年后，她嫁给了鲁珀特王子。

电脑怪杰兄弟智囊团把他们的公司开在了城堡里，公司提供最先进的安保系统。他们的专属产品是利蒂西娅王后探测器，完全可以保证使用者的人身安全。六兄弟也一起幸福地生活到老！

全剧终

公主和青蛙

布景和道具

布景：整场话剧发生在一座城堡的花园里。剪掉硬纸箱的箱底、箱顶和箱子一侧，作为许愿池。箱子外表面画上砖头图案，面朝观众。确保弗雷德里克可以从箱子里钻进钻出。再摆放几盆真花或者假花装扮花园。

道具：1号青蛙需要谱架和一根木棍作为指挥棒。用硬纸板做出圆形的太阳和月亮，把它们粘在上好色的木棍上。莉莉公主的球要又亮又好看。用硬纸板做出一张巨大的红色嘴唇，也粘在上好色的木棍上。用硬纸板做出"嗖的一下！"的闪亮标志，标志要正好能盖住跪着的弗雷德里克。

演员表

旁白：讲故事的人。

弗雷德里克：一只被施了魔法的青蛙。

莉莉公主：国王的独生女。

1号青蛙：青蛙合唱团的指挥。

2号青蛙：青蛙合唱团的团员。

青蛙合唱团：至少要有三只青蛙，但是，没有上限，所以，你想怎么安排都可以！

妆容和服装

旁白：衬衫和裤子，配披肩。

弗雷德里克：绿衣、绿裤和大号塑料眼镜、青蛙头饰。

弗雷德里克的狗：上衣为棕色或黑色，配上用人造皮做的狗耳朵样式的发卡。

莉莉公主：漂亮的裙子。

1号青蛙：绿衣、绿裤和青蛙头饰。

2号青蛙：绿衣、绿裤和青蛙头饰。

青蛙合唱团：绿衣、绿裤和青蛙头饰。

舞台方位

右侧幕区 左侧幕区

上舞台右侧 上舞台中心 上舞台左侧
舞台正位右侧 舞台正位 舞台正位左侧
下舞台右侧 下舞台中心 下舞台左侧

Script: The Princess and the Frog

Scene 1: The Castle Garden

(Opening Curtain: Narrator sits at stage right. The wishing well is at center stage with a music stand in front of it. The Frog Chorus hops on and kneels at downstage center.)

Narrator: Once upon a time, a very long time ago, there was a princess.

Frederick: *(Enters stage left)* What about me?

Narrator: I'll get to your part in a minute. As I was saying, once upon a time there was a princess—a very beautiful princess, in fact.

Frederick: And a very handsome frog.

Narrator: *(Turning to look at him)* Actually, you are a very clever frog. And, if you remember, there are quite a few other frogs in this story.

Frederick: I'm the only important one.

Frog Chorus: *(Angrily)* Hey!

Narrator: That's your opinion. All frogs are important!

Frog Chorus: *(Put right fists in the air)* Yes!

Narrator: Now, all of you important frogs need to sit
quietly while I tell this story. *(Pointing at Frederick)* You
sit over there! And the rest of you sit over there!

(All frogs sigh very loudly. The Frog Chorus sits down

in a semi-circle around the well facing the audience. Frederick stands to one side.)

Frederick: *(Tapping his foot loudly)* It's very hard to wait.

Narrator: *(Ignoring him)* Now, the king of the land was a very powerful man. His daughter, Lily, had everything she could ever wish for.

Frederick: *(Throwing his hands out dramatically)* Except for a frog.

(Princess walks in from stage left. A member of the stage crew follows her with the sun.)

Narrator: One afternoon, Princess Lily was walking in the garden.

Frederick: *(Holding up a finger)* Wait a minute! It was evening and she was playing with her ball.

Narrator: *(Angrily)* Would you like to tell the story?

Frederick: I'd love to! I've never understood why stories need a narrator anyway. Why don't you just sit over there! *(Pointing)*

Narrator: *(Sits on the edge of the stage)* Whatever!

(Princess and the stage crew with the sun exit the stage looking annoyed. Curtains close.)

剧本：公主和青蛙

第一幕：城堡的花园里

（大幕拉开：旁白坐在舞台右边。许愿池放在舞台中央，前边立一个谱架。青蛙合唱团蹦跳着上台，跪在下舞台中心。）

旁白：很久很久以前，有一位公主。

弗雷德里克：（从舞台左侧上场）怎么不说说我呢？

旁白：马上就讲到你。我刚才说什么来着，噢，很久很久以前，有一位——美貌绝伦的公主。

弗雷德里克：和一只英俊无比的青蛙。

旁白：（转身看着青蛙）你的确是只聪明绝顶的青蛙。不过，要是我没记错的话，这个故事里还有一些别的青蛙呢。

弗雷德里克：可是，我是那只最重要的。

青蛙合唱团：（生气地）嘿！瞧瞧你说什么哪！

旁白：这不过是你的看法罢了。每只青蛙都很重要啊！

青蛙合唱团：（右手挥拳）说得对！

旁白：好了，所有重要的青蛙，在我讲故事的时候，都要安静地坐好哟。(指着弗雷德里克) 你坐到那边去！其他的青蛙坐到那儿！

(所有的青蛙都大声叹气。青蛙合唱团在许愿池旁围成半个圈坐好，面向观众。弗雷德里克站在一边。)

弗雷德里克：(脚用力点着地面，发出巨大的声音) 我可等不及了。

旁白：(忽略他的抱怨) 那时，国王是这片土地上权力最大的人。他的女儿——莉莉，想要什么就可以得到什么。

弗雷德里克：(夸张地伸出手) 除了一只青蛙。

(公主从舞台左边上场。一名舞台工作人员举着太阳跟在后面。)

旁白：一天下午，莉莉公主在花园里散步。

弗雷德里克：(伸出一根手指) 等一下！原来的故事是说，"一天晚上，她在花园里玩球。"

旁白：(生气地说) 要不你来讲故事？

弗雷德里克：求之不得呢！我真不明白，干吗要请个旁白来讲故事呢？你坐在那边，怎么样？(手指远方)

55

旁白：（坐在舞台边上）唉，爱怎么样就怎么样吧！

（公主和举着太阳的舞台工作人员略显生气地下场。

大幕拉上。）

show出你的发音
争当英语小明星
▶ 地道口语课
▶ 剧本推荐

微信扫码

Scene 2: The Castle Garden

(Curtains open. Frederick is wearing the narrator's cloak. The princess enters from stage left followed by a stage crew member with the moon.)

Frederick: Once upon a time there was a beautiful princess. One evening, she was playing with her ball in the castle garden. It was almost dark and the full moon shone brightly. She could hear the frogs singing by the wishing well. *(Points to Frog Chorus)* Okay guys, you're on!

Frog Chorus: *(The Chorus is divided into three sections. The first says* peep, peep. *The second says* croak, croak. *The third says* chirr-ump, chirr-ump. *Each part follows the first with no pause in between. As each section sings, the frogs in that section should stand up and then sit down immediately. Frog #1 is the director. He taps a stick against his music stand, clears his throat and then holds the stick up as a signal for the Frog Chorus to begin.)* Peep, peep, croak, croak, chirr-ump, chirr-ump. *(Repeat three times.)*

Frederick: Just then a handsome frog entered the garden. *(Frederick whips off his cloak and throws it to the narrator.)* Ribbit, ribbit!

Frog #1: *(Holds up his hand for the others to stop singing)* Whoa, you're not from around here, are you?

Frederick: *(Swaggering toward them)* No, I'm not. In fact, my name is Sir Frederick!

(The Frog Chorus gasps.)

Frog #2: But, you look like a frog!

Frederick: Looks can be deceiving. What if I told you that I've been enchanted by an evil sorceress?

(The Frog Chorus gasps again and backs away.)

Frederick: Don't worry! She lives far away in another kingdom. I doubt she will ever visit your little garden. But someday I will live in a castle again and eat every meal with a beautiful princess.

Frog #1: I'm really sorry. I had no idea who you were. You look like an ordinary, little, green frog. Is there anything we can do to help you?

Frederick: I'm afraid you can't help me. *(He points to the princess.)* But, Princess Lily can. I just have to convince her to kiss me.

Frog #1: *(Looks disgusted)* She's not going to kiss you!

Frederick: Yes, she will. Sing your song again. Maybe she'll come a little closer.

Frog #2: I really liked that song you were singing.

Frederick: That's what all the frogs sing in my kingdom. Repeat after me. Ribbit, ribbit!

Frog Chorus: Peep, peep, croak, croak, chirr-ump, chirr-ump. *(Then all say together.)* Ribbit, ribbit! *(Repeat three times.)*

Princess Lily: *(Moving nearer)* That's odd. The frogs sound different tonight!

Frog Chorus: Peep, peep, croak, croak, chirr-ump, chirr-ump, ribbit, ribbit! *(Repeat three times.)*

Princess: I wonder what's wrong with them.

(Frog Chorus should continue to sing quietly in the background.)

Princess: *(Throws her ball in the air and catches it)* Oh dear, I wish I had someone to play with. It's not much fun playing ball alone.

Frederick: Here is my chance to speak to the princess!

Frog #1: *(Rushing over and whispering)* Stop, Sir Frederick! Frogs aren't supposed to speak to princesses!

Frederick: Why not?

Frog #2: Because we are *frogs*.

Frederick: I've never heard of anything so silly! Everyone should be allowed to speak to everyone else. Anyway, I'm not really a frog. *(Bowing deeply and then sitting down)* Your majesty, allow me to introduce myself. I am Sir Frederick and I would love to play ball with you.

Princess: *(Looking around)* Who said that?

Frederick: Me, I'm down here by your feet.

Princess: Ewww! You're nothing but a nasty, little, green frog. I was hoping for a handsome prince.

Frederick: Then it's your lucky day! I'm not really a frog. An evil sorceress cast a spell on me!

Princess: *(Hands on hips)* That only happens in fairy tales! I don't believe you.

Frederick: Oh well, it was worth a try. Can we still play ball, please?

Princess: Never mind, I'm not interested in playing with a frog. I'll just throw the ball myself. *(Waving her hand)* Why don't you hop off somewhere?

Frederick: *(Bowing)* As you wish.

Princess: *(Throws ball into the well)* Oh no! My ball went into the well. *(Looking down)* I can't even see it. The water is too deep. That was my favorite ball. *(She begins to cry and then looks up.)* Frog? Where are you?

Frederick: Please call me *Sir Frederick*. Can I be of service?

Princess: I lost my ball in the well. Could you swim down and get it for me?

Frederick: Of course, I can. But why would I want to? You haven't been very nice to me.

Princess: I'm sorry. I have never talked to a frog before.

Frederick: Well, frogs have feelings too, just like everyone else. You think you are special just because you are a princess.

Princess: I apologized. What more do you want?

Frederick: *(Rubbing chin)* Let me see, maybe you could give me some kind of reward.

Princess: *(Sighing loudly)* I suppose you want a kiss? Ewww!

Frederick: Oh no. I was thinking more of a condo or a sports car.

Princess: *What?!* Just for getting my ball out of the well? You have *got* to be kidding!

Frederick: Perhaps you could just let me live in the castle with you. I could eat at your table and sleep in your room.

Princess: You ask too much.

Frederick: Well, then how about a kiss? I'll settle for that.

Princess: Well . . .

Frederick: *(Looking down into the well)* That water is very deep. You'll never see that ball again without my help.

Princess: Oh all right, you nasty thing! Find my ball and I'll give you a kiss!

Frederick: At your service! I'll only be a moment! *(Frederick enters well from behind and ducks down below the cardboard.)*

第二幕：城堡的花园里

（大幕拉开，弗雷德里克披上旁白的披风。公主从舞台左侧上场。一名舞台工作人员举着月亮跟在后面。）

弗雷德里克：很久很久以前，有一位美貌绝伦的公主。一天晚上，她在城堡的花园里玩球。夜很深了，皎洁的月光洒向地面。公主听到了来自许愿池旁青蛙的歌声。（手指青蛙合唱团）好了，伙计们，现在轮到你们了！

青蛙合唱团：（合唱团分成三组：第一组发出"唧唧"的声音，第二组发出"呱呱"的声音，第三组发出"咕儿——呱，咕儿——呱"的声音。三组声音转换应衔接好，没有停顿。每组唱歌时，应起立，唱完立刻坐下。1号青蛙是指挥。他先用指挥棒敲一敲谱架，清一清嗓子，然后举起指挥棒，给合唱团发出"开始"的信号。）唧唧，呱呱，咕儿——呱，咕儿——呱。（按照这个顺序重复三遍。）

弗雷德里克：正在这时，一只英俊无比的青蛙来到了花园。(弗雷德里克迅速取下披风，扔到旁白那儿。) 蝈蝈，蝈蝈！

1号青蛙：（伸手叫停合唱团）喔，你不是这儿的青蛙吧？

弗雷德里克：(傲慢地冲着合唱团说) 当然不是啦。我，其实是弗雷德里克男爵！

（青蛙合唱团吓了一跳。）

2号青蛙：不过，你看起来就像只青蛙啊！

弗雷德里克：你们看到的，并不见得是真的。如果我告诉你，我是被巫婆施了魔法才变成这样的，你会不会信？

（青蛙合唱团吓得后退几步。）

弗雷德里克：别担心！那个巫婆住在一个特别遥远的地方。我觉得，她是不会到你们这个小花园来的。不过，有一天，我会再次住回城堡里，跟美丽的公主共餐。

1号青蛙：我真的很同情你的遭遇。不过，我实在想象不出来，你到底是谁。其实，你看上去就是一只又小又绿、再平常不过的青蛙。我们可以帮你做点儿什么呢？

弗雷德里克：我估计，你们帮不了我的。(指向公主)
不过，莉莉公主倒可以帮上忙。我得说服她亲我一口。

1号青蛙：(厌恶地看着弗雷德里克)她才不会亲你呢！

弗雷德里克：会的，她会的。你们唱起来吧。她没准
会往这边走的。

2号青蛙：我其实挺喜欢你刚才唱的那首歌的。

弗雷德里克：这才是我的王国里的青蛙应该唱的呢。
来，跟我唱。蝈蝈，蝈蝈！

青蛙合唱团：唧唧，呱呱，咕儿——呱，咕儿——呱。
(三组一起。)蝈蝈，蝈蝈！(重复三遍。)

莉莉公主：(向这边靠近)真奇怪，今晚的青蛙叫听
起来挺特别啊！

青蛙合唱团：唧唧，呱呱，咕儿——呱，咕儿——呱。
蝈蝈，蝈蝈！(重复三遍。)

莉莉公主：我觉得，这些青蛙有点儿不对劲。

(青蛙合唱团继续唱，但是，声音变弱作为背景音。)

莉莉公主：(把球抛向空中，再接住)唉，真想找人
跟我玩。自己玩球太没意思了。

弗雷德里克：现在，我有和公主搭话的机会了！

1号青蛙：（冲到弗雷德里克旁边，小声说）弗雷德里克男爵，等一下！青蛙是不可以和公主说话的呀！

弗雷德里克：为什么不可以呀？

2号青蛙：因为，我们只是青蛙啊。

弗雷德里克：我从来没有听过这么荒唐的事儿！每个人都有和别人交谈的权利。再说了，我真不是一只普通的青蛙。

（深鞠躬，蹲下）尊敬的陛下，请允许我做一下自我介绍。我是弗雷德里克男爵，我，想和您一起玩球。

莉莉公主：（向四周看看）谁在说话？

弗雷德里克：我啊，我就在您脚下呀！

莉莉公主：哎呀！你不过是一只又小又脏的绿青蛙罢了。我想找位英俊的王子来玩球。

弗雷德里克：那，您再幸运不过了！我其实不是一只普通的青蛙。我是被一个巫婆施了魔法的！

莉莉公主：（双手叉腰）这种事，只会发生在童话故事里！我才不相信你呢。

弗雷德里克：好吧，虽然您不相信我，但事实确实如此。那，就让我们来玩球吧，拜托！

莉莉公主：算了吧，我可没兴趣和一只青蛙玩。我还是自己玩吧。（摆摆手）你跳到别处去，好吗？

弗雷德里克：（鞠躬）好吧，如您所愿。

莉莉公主：（把球扔进了井里）哦，天哪！我的球掉进井里了。（向井深处看去）我根本看不见它了，水太深了。这可是我最喜欢的球啊。（她哭了起来，然后抬头看。）青蛙，你在哪儿啊？

弗雷德里克：请叫我弗雷德里克男爵。有什么可以为您效劳的吗？

莉莉公主：我的球掉进井里了。你能不能游下去把它捞上来？

弗雷德里克：当然可以了。不过，我为什么要帮助您呢？您刚才对我的态度一点儿都不友好。

莉莉公主：很抱歉。我从来没和青蛙说过话。

弗雷德里克：嗯，青蛙和其他人一样，也是有感情的呀。就因为您是公主，所以您才觉得自己那么与众不同。

莉莉公主：我为我说过的话向你道歉。你还想怎样？

弗雷德里克：（抚摸着下巴）让我想想啊，或许，您能回报我点儿什么。

莉莉公主：（大声叹气）我猜，你想从我这儿要个吻吧？哎呀！

弗雷德里克：噢，这倒不是。我不过想要栋公寓或者跑车什么的。

莉莉公主：什么？！你只不过给我捞个球罢了！别开玩笑了！

弗雷德里克：或者，你可以让我和你一起住在城堡里。我可以在你的桌子上吃饭，还可以睡在你的房间里。

莉莉公主：你的要求太过分了。

弗雷德里克：真的吗？那就来个吻吧。我就降低下我的要求呗。

莉莉公主：这个……

弗雷德里克：（向井里望了望）这水可真深啊。要是没有我的帮助，你可就再也见不到你的球啦。

莉莉公主：哎呀，好吧，你这个讨厌鬼！去给我把球捞上来，然后，我会给你一个吻！

弗雷德里克：愿意为您效劳！我马上就回来！（弗雷德里克从许愿池道具后进入，在纸板后低下身子。）

Scene 3: The Castle Garden

Narrator: Just a few minutes later . . .

Princess: *(Looking down into the well)* That frog has been gone a long time. What if he can't find it?

Narrator: *(Stepping forward)* Don't worry, he will.

Princess: How do you know?

Narrator: I'm the narrator. I know the whole story.

Frederick: *(Appearing with the ball)* Whew! Your ball was a long way down!

Princess: Ewww! It's all wet and muddy!

Frederick: So am I! Pucker up!

Princess: *(Backing away)* Wait! Wait! Wait! Let me think. Isn't there something else that you want?

Frederick: Sure! I'd settle for a really nice condo on the fifteenth floor with a view of the river. Or, I'd love a little red sports car with real leather seats!

Princess: You are ridiculous! Do you still want to live with me at the castle?

Frederick: *(Hopping up and down happily)* Yes! Yes! Can I eat at your table and sleep in your room?

Princess: For how long?

Frederick: For the rest of my life!

Narrator: I wonder how long *that* will be.

Princess: *(Disgusted)* I can't do that!

Frederick: Then you'll have to kiss me.

Princess: *(Sighs)* Oh, all right.

(Frederick hops up closer to her.)

Princess: Wait! Narrator, I have to know . . . is this frog really a handsome prince in disguise?

Narrator: Not exactly, but he isn't a frog either.

Princess: *(Sighs)* Some people have the worst luck! Come here, Frederick! *(Princess kisses Frederick using huge pink lips on a paint stick.)*

第三幕：城堡的花园里

旁白：几分钟过后……

莉莉公主：（向井里张望）那只青蛙已经进去好长时间了。要是他找不到球该怎么办啊？

旁白：（向前走一步）别着急，他一定会把球捞上来的。

莉莉公主：你怎么知道啊？

旁白：我是旁白啊，整个故事我都知道。

弗雷德里克：（出现在井边，手里拿着球）哟嘿！你的球掉得还挺深的！

莉莉公主：哎哟！！我的球那么湿，全是泥巴！

弗雷德里克：我浑身上下也湿透了，粘的都是泥啊！好了，噘起嘴来！

莉莉公主：（往后退几步）等一下！等一下！等一下！让我再考虑考虑吧。还有没有什么别的东西是你想要的呢？

弗雷德里克：有啊！要是给我一栋十五层以上的河景公寓，也不错哟！再不然，给我一辆有真皮座椅的红色跑车吧！

莉莉公主：太荒唐了！你还要和我住在城堡里吗？

弗雷德里克：(快乐地跳上跳下) 要啊！要啊！能不能坐在你的桌子上吃饭、睡在你的房间里啊？

莉莉公主：那……要多久呢？

弗雷德里克：我下半辈子都要这样啊！

旁白：我在想，他的"下半辈子"有多长。

莉莉公主：(厌恶地说) 我可不想这么做！

弗雷德里克：那您就得亲我一下。

莉莉公主：(叹口气) 唉，那好吧。

(弗雷德里克跳起，试着靠近她)

莉莉公主：等一下！旁白，我想知道……这只青蛙，真是位英俊的王子变的吗？

旁白：嗯……不完全是你想象的那样，不过，他也不是一只普通的青蛙。

莉莉公主：(叹口气) 有的人的运气真的挺差的！到这儿来吧，弗雷德里克。(公主用带有木棍的嘴唇道具亲了弗雷德里克一下。)

Scene 4: The Castle Garden

(Stage crew covers Frederick with a big cardboard sign that says POOF! Frederick the dog takes his place.)

Narrator: A few minutes later . . .

Frederick: Bark! Bark!

Princess: You aren't a prince. You're a dog! *(Frederick takes the ball from her hand and runs on his hands and knees across the stage toward Frog #1.)*

Frog #1: Wow, Frederick! Why didn't you tell us?

Frederick: I told you I was under a spell from an evil sorceress. I belonged to a princess in another kingdom, but now I'll never get back home. It took a kiss from another princess to turn back into a dog again.

Princess: *(Clapping happily)* I can't believe you're a dog! I've always wanted a dog! We can play ball in the garden, and you can live in the castle and sleep in my room! I'm so excited!

Narrator: And the princess and the frog—I mean dog—lived happily ever after.

Frog Chorus: Peep, peep, croak, croak, chirr-ump, chirr-ump, ribbit, ribbit! *(Say only once.)*

The End

第四幕：城堡的花园里

（舞台工作人员用一个带有"嗖的一下！"标志的纸板罩住弗雷德里克。小狗弗雷德里克出现在舞台上。）

旁白：几分钟过后……

弗雷德里克：汪汪！汪汪！

莉莉公主：你不是王子啊，你怎么是只狗啊？（弗雷德里克从她的手里抢过球，用膝盖和手爬到1号青蛙的身边。）

1号青蛙：哇，弗雷德里克！你之前为什么没告诉我们你是只狗啊？

弗雷德里克：我告诉你们了啊，我说，一个巫婆给我施了魔法。我是属于那个王国的公主的，可是，我再也回不去了。现在，一个公主的吻让我又变回了狗。

莉莉公主：（高兴地拍手）真不敢相信，你是只狗啊！我一直想要一只小狗的！我们可以一起在花园里玩球，你还可以住在城堡里，睡在我的房间里！这太让我兴奋了！

旁白：于是，公主和青蛙——哦不，我是指和这只狗过上了幸福的生活，一直到永远。

青蛙合唱团：唧唧，呱呱，咕儿——呱，咕儿——呱。（三组一起。）蝈蝈，蝈蝈！（只唱一遍。）

全剧终

show出你的发音
争当英语小明星
▶ 地道口语课
▶ 剧本推荐

微信扫码